PIANO · VOCAL

RODGERS & ROMANCE

LOVE SONGS BY RICHARD RODGERS

Cover: Richard Rodgers (1959), Photo by Toni Frissell

ISBN 0-7935-8955-X

www.williamsonmusic.com

EXCLUSIVELY DISTRIBUTED BY

HAL•LEONARD® CORPORATION

7777 W. BLUEMOUND RD. P.O. BOX 13819 MILWAUKEE, WI 53213

Visit Hal Leonard Online at
www.halleonard.com

Contents

RICHARD RODGERS

A Brief Biography

Richard Rodgers' contributions to the musical theatre of his day were extraordinary, and his influence on the musical theatre of today and tomorrow is legendary. His career spanned more than six decades, and his hits ranged from the silver screens of Hollywood to the bright lights of Broadway, London and beyond. He was the recipient of countless awards, including Pulitzers, Tonys, Oscars, Grammys and Emmys. He wrote more than 900 published songs, and forty Broadway musicals.

Richard Charles Rodgers was born in New York City on June 28, 1902. His earliest professional credits, beginning in 1920, included a series of musicals for Broadway, London and Hollywood written exclusively with lyricist Lorenz Hart. In the first decade of their collaboration, Rodgers and Hart averaged two new shows every season, beginning with *Poor Little Ritz Girl*, and also including *The Garrick Gaieties* (of 1925 and 1926), *Dearest Enemy, Peggy-Ann, A Connecticut Yankee* and *Chee-Chee*. After spending the years 1931 to 1935 in Hollywood (where they wrote the scores for several feature films including *Love Me Tonight* starring Maurice Chevalier, *Hallelujah, I'm a Bum* starring Al Jolson and *The Phantom President* starring George M. Cohan), they returned to New York to compose the score for Billy Rose's circus extravaganza, *Jumbo*.

A golden period followed — golden for Rodgers & Hart, and golden for the American musical: *On Your Toes* (1936), *Babes in Arms* (1937), *I'd Rather Be Right* (1937), *I Married an Angel* (1938), *The Boys from Syracuse* (1938), *Too Many Girls* (1939), *Higher and Higher* (1940), *Pal Joey* (1940), and *By Jupiter* (1942). The Rodgers & Hart partnership came to an end with the death of Lorenz Hart in 1943, at the age of 48.

Earlier that year Rodgers had joined forces with lyricist and author Oscar Hammerstein II, whose work in the field of operetta throughout the '20s and '30s had been as innovative as Rodgers' own accomplishments in the field of musical comedy. *Oklahoma!* (1943), the first Rodgers and Hammerstein musical, was also the first of a new genre, the musical play, representing a unique fusion of Rodgers' musical comedy and Hammerstein's operetta. A milestone in the development of the American musical, it also marked the beginning of the most successful partnership in Broadway musical history, and was followed by *Carousel* (1945), *Allegro* (1947), *South Pacific* (1949), *The King and I* (1951), *Me and Juliet* (1953), *Pipe Dream* (1955), *Flower Drum Song* (1958) and *The Sound of Music* (1959). The team wrote one movie musical, *State Fair* (1945), and one for television, *Cinderella* (1957). Collectively, the Rodgers & Hammerstein musicals earned 34 Tony Awards, 15 Academy Awards, two Pulitzer Prizes, two Grammy Awards and an Emmy Award. In 1998, Rodgers & Hammerstein were cited by Time Magazine and CBS News as among the 20 most influential artists & entertainers of the 20th Century. In 1999 they were commemorated in a U.S. postage stamp.

Despite Hammerstein's death in 1960, Rodgers continued to write for the Broadway stage. His first solo entry, *No Strings* in 1962, earned him two Tony Awards for music and lyrics, and was followed by *Do I Hear a Waltz?* (1965, lyrics by Stephen Sondheim), *Two by Two* (1970, lyrics by Martin Charnin), *Rex* (1976, lyrics by Sheldon Harnick) and *I Remember Mama* (1979, lyrics by Martin Charnin and Raymond Jessel).

No Strings was not the only project for which Rodgers worked solo: as composer/lyricist he wrote the score for a 1967 television adaptation of Bernard Shaw's *Androcles and the Lion* for NBC; contributed songs to a 1962 remake of *State Fair*; and to the 1965 movie version of *The Sound of Music*. He composed one ballet score (*Ghost Town*, premiered in 1939), and two television documentary scores—*Victory at Sea* in 1952 and *The Valiant Years* in 1960 (the former earning him an Emmy, a Gold Record and a commendation from the U.S. Navy.)

Richard Rodgers died at home in New York City on December 30, 1979 at the age of 77. On March 27, 1990, he was honored posthumously with Broadway's highest accolade when the 46th Street Theatre, owned and operated by the Nederlander Organization, was renamed The Richard Rodgers Theatre, home to The Richard Rodgers Gallery, a permanent exhibit in the lobby areas presented by ASCAP which honors the composer's life and works.

To learn more, visit:
www.rnh.com

ALL AT ONCE YOU LOVE HER

from PIPE DREAM

Lyrics by OSCAR HAMMERSTEIN II
Music by RICHARD RODGERS

C7
F
dream will take pos - ses - sion of your heart.
Refrain (slowly, with expression)
F
C7
mp
You start to light her cig - ar - ette
And all at once you love her.
F
You've scarce - ly talked,

C7
you've scarce - ly met,
But all at once you
A7
Dm
B♭
love
her.
You like her eyes,
mf
F
Dm7
F6
G9
you tell her so.
She thinks you're wise and
cresc.
G7
C7
F
clev - er.
You kiss good - night
mp

C7
and then you know
You'll kiss good-night for-
E♭maj7/F
F7
B♭
B♭/A
Gm7
ev - er.
You won - der where,
F
B♭9
F
C7
your heart can go
Then all at once you
F
B♭/C
C7
F
know.
know.

AWAY FROM YOU

from REX

Lyrics by SHELDON HARNICK
Music by RICHARD RODGERS

C7
F
Dm
G
C
and time's a trav - 'ler who's lost his way.
The
the fields are thirst - y; the streams are dry.
We
F
Gm
Gm7
C7
F7
peo - ple I meet might as well be stat - ues,
the
live, you and I, for an hour of sun - light,
so
B♭
Dm
G7
C9sus
C7
words we ex - change might as well be Greek.
The
brief an es - cape from a world of gray.
Our
Fm
C/E
room that I'm in may be bright and cheer - ful
but to
mo - ments of warmth have been touch and go, love,
but to -

Am
Am7
D7
G9sus
Gdim7
G7
me it's dim and bleak.
I'm
night we'll touch and stay.
I'm
Cdim7
C
Dm
G
C7
F
half a - live un - til the mo - ment the door swings o - pen
half a - live un - til the mo - ment the door swings o - pen
1
F/E
Dm7
G7sus
G7
Cdim7
C
C7
and you walk through; and so you see why I can
F
E7
Am
Fm6
C/G
G7
Cdim7
C
nev - er be a - way from you.

Cdim7
C
2
G7
F
A - and you walk through.
Now my soul is a - float
C/E
Am
D7
on a wave of mu - sic!
That I could feel such joy,
I nev - er
G9sus
G7
Cdim7
C
C7
F
E7
knew!
And so you see why I can nev - er
Am
Fm6
C/G
G7
C6
C
Cdim7 C
be a - way from you.

BEWITCHED

from PAL JOEY

Words by LORENZ HART
Music by RICHARD RODGERS

Dm7
G7
Cmaj7
C6
Dm7
G7
Since this half - pint im - i - ta - tion, Put me on the blink. I'm
rit.
Slowly
C
G7/D
C/E
C+/E
wild a - gain, be - guiled a - gain, a sim - per - ing, whim - per - ing
p a tempo
F
Ddim7
C/E
D7
G7
A7
child a - gain, Be - witched, both - ered and be - wil - dered am
Dm
G7
C
G7/D
I. Could - n't sleep, and would - n't sleep, When
mf
p

C/E C+/E F Ddim7 C/E D7
love came and told me I should-n't sleep, Be - witched, both-ered and be -
G7 C7 F A7
wil - dered am I.
Dm Dm7 Am
Lost my heart, but what of it? He is cold, I a -
mp
Dm7 G7 Dm7/G G7
gree, He can laugh, but I love it, Al-though the

Em7
E♭dim7
Dm7
G7
C
laugh's on me. I'll sing to him, each
mf
p
G7/D
C/E
C+/E
F
Ddim7
spring to him, And long for the day when I'll cling to him, Be -
C/E
D7
G9
1
C
Am
witched, both - ered and be - wil - dered am I.
Dm7
G7
2
C
F
C6
I'm I.
sf

BLUE MOON

Words by LORENZ HART
Music by RICHARD RODGERS

Cmaj9
C6
Dm7
G7sus
G7
C(add9)
C
up for I went to sleep at ten.
sev - en Hat - ing the morn - ing light.
rit.
Fm7
A♭/B♭
B♭7
E♭maj7
E♭6
Cm7
F7
Fm7/B♭
B♭7
Life was a bit - ter cup for the sad - dest of all men.
Now I a - wake in Heav - en and all the world's all right.
Blue
Slowly, with feeling
E♭
Cm
Fm7
B♭7
moon you saw me stand - ing a - lone
p
sim.
Fm
Eb
With - out a dream in my heart,
With - out a love of my own;
3fr

Eb
Ab
Eb/G
Bb7/F
Bb7
Cm
Fm7
Fm7/Bb
Ab6
Bb13
3 fr
4 fr
5 fr
Blue moon you knew just what I was there for you heard me say-ing a pray'r for some-one I real-ly could care for
And then there sud-den-ly ap-peared be-fore me
The on-ly one my arms will ev-er hold
I heard some-
mf

A♭m
D♭7
G♭
B♭/F
Cm7/F
F7
bod - y whis-per, "Please a - dore me" And when I looked, the moon had turned to
F♭m7/B♭
B♭7
E♭
Cm
Fm7
B♭7
E♭
Cm
gold! Blue moon! Now I'm no long-er a - lone
p
sim.
Fm7
B♭
E♭
Cm
Fm7
Fm7/B♭
With - out a dream in my heart, With-out a love of my own.
1
E♭
A♭
E♭
B♭7
2
E♭
A♭
E♭
Blue
mf

THE BLUE ROOM
from THE GIRL FRIEND

Words by LORENZ HART
Music by RICHARD RODGERS

B♭
Fmaj7
B♭
F
broth - er's room, On the wall are two prints.
B♭
F
D7
Gm
3fr
D7
Here's the kid - dies' room, Here's the
8va
Gm
3fr
D7
Gm7
3fr
C7
bid - dy's room, Here's a pan - try lined with
F6
C7
Fmaj7
B♭
Fmaj7
shelves, dear, Here I've planned for us, Some - thing

B♭ Fmaj7 B♭ B♭maj7/A Gm7 C7
grand for us, Where we two can be our - selves, dear,
rall.
Slowly, with expression
F C7 F
We'll have a blue room, a new room, For
C7 F Fmaj7 F7 B♭ Gm7
two room, Where ev - 'ry day's a hol - i - day Be -
F G7 C7 F
cause you're mar - ried to me. Not like a

C7
F
C7
ball - room A small room, A hall room, Where
F
Fmaj7
F7
B♭
Gm7
3 fr
F
Gm7
3 fr
C7
I
you
can smoke
my
your
pipe a - way, With
your
my
wee head up - on
my
your
F
C7
knee. We will thrive on, keep a - live on
L.H.
F
C7
Just noth - ing but kiss - es, With Mis - ter and

Gm7
3 fr
C7
Dm7
G7
C7
Mis - sus On lit - tle blue chairs.
F
C7
F
You sew your
I'll wear my
trous - seau, And Rob - in - son
C7
F
Fmaj7
F7
B♭
Gm7
Cru - soe Is not so far from world - ly cares As our
F
Gm7
C7
1
F
Gm7
C7
2
F
blue room far a - way up - stairs!
stairs!
poco rall.
rit.

BOYS AND GIRLS LIKE YOU AND ME

cut from OKLAHOMA!

Lyrics by OSCAR HAMMERSTEIN II
Music by RICHARD RODGERS

Fm Bb Fm Bb C7 Fm
year to year, Be - liev - ing in each oth - er, as we do,
C C+ Dm7 G9 C
Brave - ly march - ing for - ward, two by two.
C7
poco rit.
Refrain
F
(slowly and with tenderness)
Boys and girls like you and me
p - mf
Gm7 C7 F6 C7
Walk be - neath the skies. They love just as
poco a poco cresc.

F C7 F Fm6 C C7

we love, With the same dream in their eyes.

Cm7 F7 Cm7 F7 B♭

Songs and kings and man - y things have their day and are

mf

B♭m6 F G7

gone, But boys and girls like you and me,

più espr. *mp*

C7 | 1 F C9 | 2 F

We go on and on. on.

mf *poco rit.* *a tempo* *f*

DANCING ON THE CEILING

from EVER GREEN

Words by LORENZ HART
Music by RICHARD RODGERS

C7♭9
F
F/A
face I see.
At night I creep in bed
A♭dim7
4fr
Gm7
3fr
F
And nev - er sleep in bed,
But look a-bove in the
air
Fm
F
C7
C7♭9
And to my great - est joy,
my
boy
is
F
Am
D7
there!
It is my prince who walks

Gm
3 fr
C7
F
In - to my dreams and talks.
He danc - es
A+
B♭6
G7
C
Em
o - ver - head on the ceil - ing, near my bed,
Gm7
3 fr
C7
F
B♭6
C7
In my sight, Through the
F
A+
night. I try to hide in vain

B♭6
G7
C
Em
Gm7
3 fr
C7
Un - der-neath my coun - ter - pane; There's my
F
B♭6
C7
F
love up a - bove!
C7
F6
I whis - per, "Go a - way, my lov - er, It's not fair,"
C7
C7♭9
But I'm so grate - ful to dis - cov - er;

F
Cdim7
C7
F
He's still there.
I love my
A+
B♭6
G7
C
Em
ceil - ing more Since it is a danc - ing floor
Gm
3 fr
C7
1
F
Just for my love.
Gm7
3 fr
C7
2
F
love.

DO I LOVE YOU BECAUSE YOU'RE BEAUTIFUL?

from CINDERELLA

Lyrics by OSCAR HAMMERSTEIN II
Music by RICHARD RODGERS

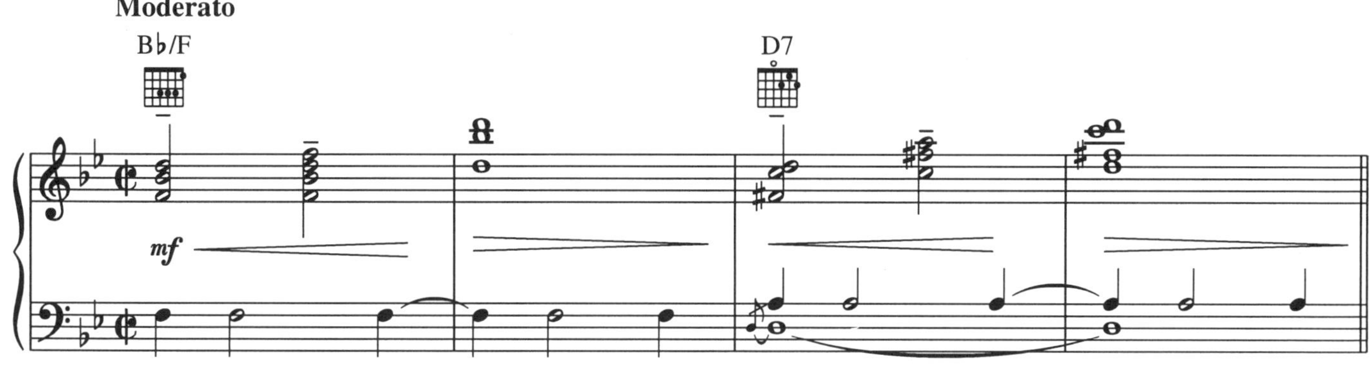

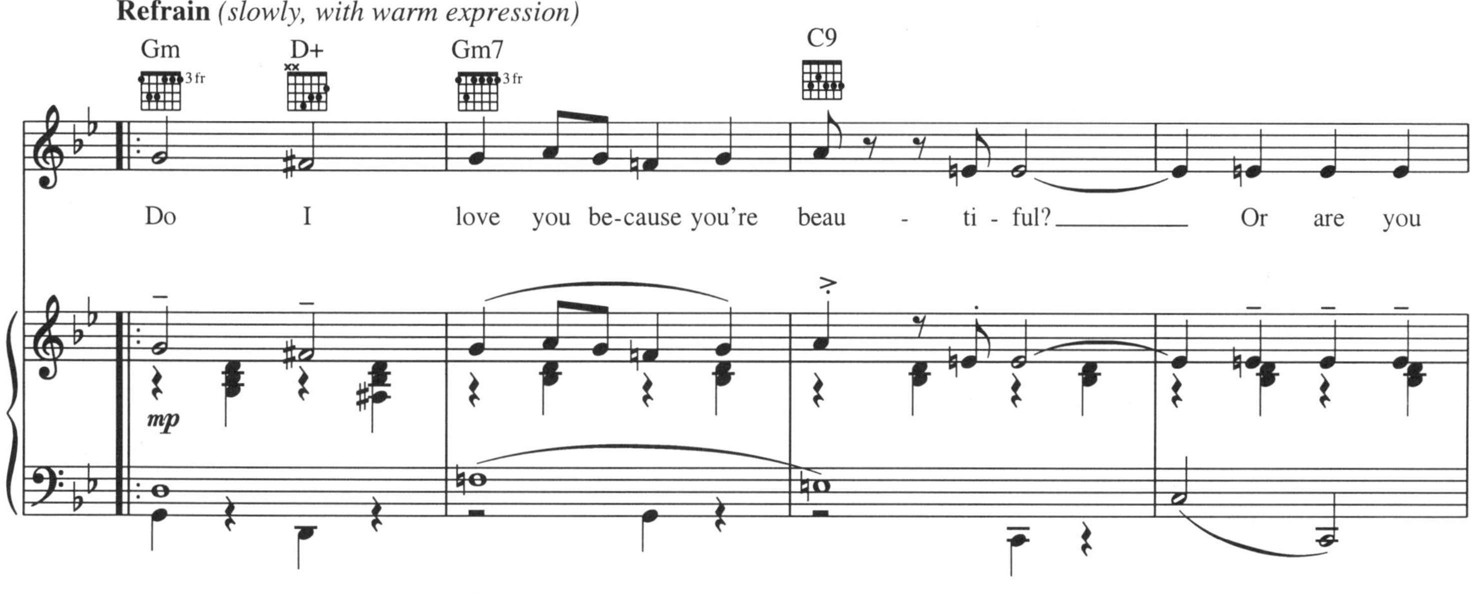

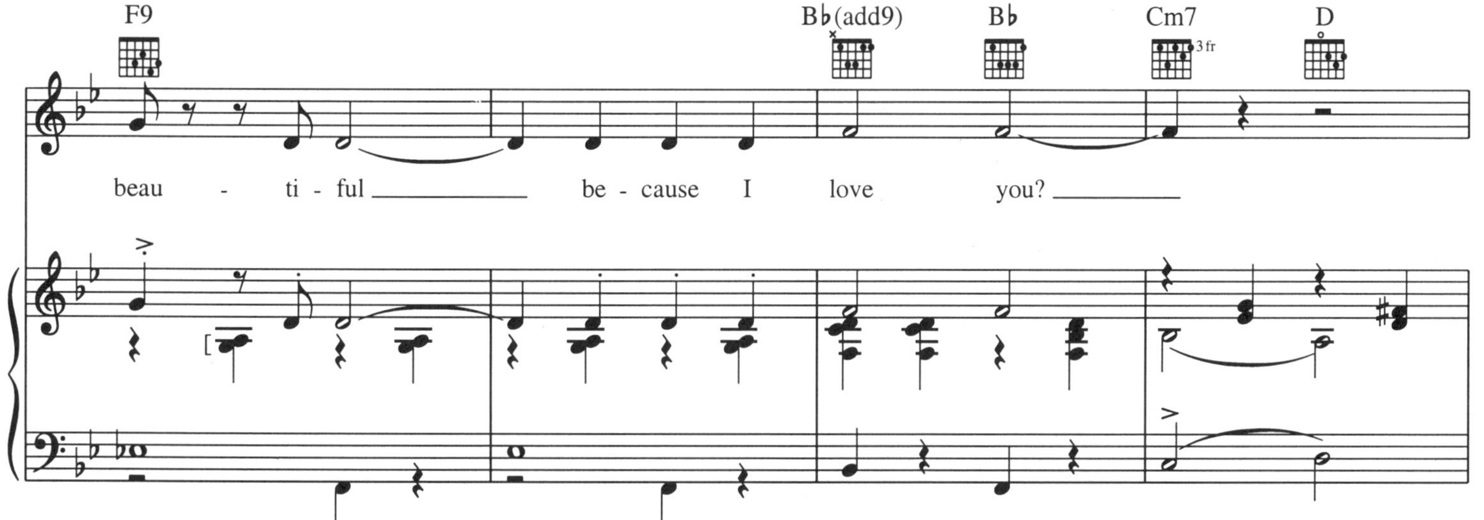

Gm
D+
Gm7
C9
Am I mak - ing be-lieve I see in you A girl too
mp
F9
Fm7/B♭
love - ly to be real - ly true?
B♭7
E♭
E♭dim7
Do I want you be - cause you're
mf espr.
B♭
B♭(add9)
B♭
Gm7
won - der - ful? Or are you won - der - ful

C9
F9
F7
D7sus
D7
Be - cause I want you?
Gm
D+/F♯
Gm7/F
C9
Are you the sweet in - ven - tion of a lov - er's dream,
mf più espr.
C7
B♭
D+
E♭
F7
Or are you real - ly as beau - ti - ful as you
f molto espr. e poco rit.
1 B♭
D7♯5
2 B♭
seem?
seem?
a tempo

FALLING IN LOVE WITH LOVE

from THE BOYS FROM SYRACUSE

Words by LORENZ HART
Music by RICHARD RODGERS

F7sus
Cm7
3 fr
F7
la - dies, let your fin - gers dance,
mf
And
F7sus
Cm7
3 fr
F7
keep your hands out of ro - mance.
Love - ly

B♭/D
G7♭9
4 fr
Cm7
3 fr
F7
witch - es, let the stitch - es Keep your
Cm7
3 fr
F7
B♭
fin - gers un - der con - trol.
Cut the
Gm
3 fr
Cm
3 fr
thread, but leave
The
Cm7
3 fr
F7
B♭
whole heart whole.

F7
Mer - ry maids can sew and sleep,
Cm7/F
Fdim7
F7
Wives can on - ly sew and weep!
B♭
B♭maj7
B♭6
B♭
Fall - ing in love with love Is fall - ing for

F7sus
F7
Cm7
3 fr
F7
make be - lieve.
F7sus
F7
F7sus
F7
Fall - ing in love with love Is play - ing the
B♭maj7
B♭6
B♭maj7
B♭6
fool;
B♭maj7
B♭6
B♭maj7
B♭6
Car - ing too much is such a ju - ve - nile

Am7
D7
F6/A
D7
fan - cy.
Gdim7
Gm
3 fr
Cm/G
3 fr
C7/G
Learn - ing to trust is just For chil - dren in
Cm7/F
Cm7
3 fr
F7
school.
B♭
B♭maj7
B♭6
B♭
I fell in love with love one night When the

F7sus
F7
Cm7
3 fr
F7
moon was full,
F7sus
F7
F7sus
F7
I was un - wise with eyes Un - a - ble to
B♭maj7
B♭6
B♭maj7
B♭6
see.
B♭maj7
B♭6
B♭maj7
B♭6
I fell in love with love, With love ev - er -

Am7
D7
Gmaj7
G7
last - ing,
But
Cm/E♭
Ddim7
Cm7
F7
3 fr
love
fell
out
with
1
B♭
F7
me.
2
B♭
B♭6
me.
Ped.
*

THE GENTLEMAN IS A DOPE

from ALLEGRO

Lyrics by OSCAR HAMMERSTEIN II
Music by RICHARD RODGERS

gen-tle-man burns me up! The gen-tle-man gets me down!
mf
R.H.
L.H.
Refrain
A7
Dm
The gen-tle-man is a dope a
p - mf leggiero
Dm6
B♭maj7
B7
man of man-y faults, A clum-sy Joe who would-n't know a
C7
F6
A7/E
Dm
Rhum-ba from a Waltz, The gen-tle-man is a dope and

G7
B♭maj7
B♭7
not my cup of tea, (Why do I get in a dith - er? He
mf
Dm/A
E7
A7
Dm
Em7
A7
Dm
does - n't be - long to me!) The gen-tle-man is - n't bright,
mf
p
Dm6
B♭maj7
he does - n't know the score A cake will come, he'll
B7
C7
F6
A7/E
Dm
take a crumb and nev - er ask for more! The gen-tle-man's eyes are blue

G7
Bb♭maj7
but lit - tle do they see (Why am I beat-ing my
mf
B♭7
Dm/A
E7
A7
Dm
Dm/C
Dm/B♭
Dm/A
D7
brains out? He does - n't be-long to me!) He's
G
G/F♯
G/E
G/D
C
C/B
C/A
C/G
some - bod - y el - se's prob - lem, She's
G
G/F♯
G/E
G/D
C9
wel - come to the guy! She'll

F F/E F/D F/C B♭ B♭/A B♭/G B♭/F
nev - er un - der - stand him half as
E7 E7♯5 E7 E7♯5 E7 A7 A7♭9 A7 A7♭9 A7 Dm
well as I. The gen-tle-man is a dope
Dm6 B♭maj7
he is - n't ver - y smart, He's just a lug you'd
B7 C7 F6 A7/E Dm
like to hug and hold a - gainst your heart. The gen-tle-man does - n't know
mf
p

G7
Bb♭maj7
How hap - py he could be.
Look at me! Cry-ing my
mf
Bb♭7
Dm/A
E7
A7
Fmaj7
Bb♭maj7
eyes out, As if he be - longed to me.
Em7(add4)
A7
D/F#
G
Ab♭7b♭5
A7
1
Dm
Em7(add4)
A7
He'll nev - er be - long to me!
The
f
mf
2
Dm6
Em7(add4)
A9
Dm
me!
f
sf
8vb

HE WAS TOO GOOD TO ME

from SIMPLE SIMON

Words by LORENZ HART
Music by RICHARD RODGERS

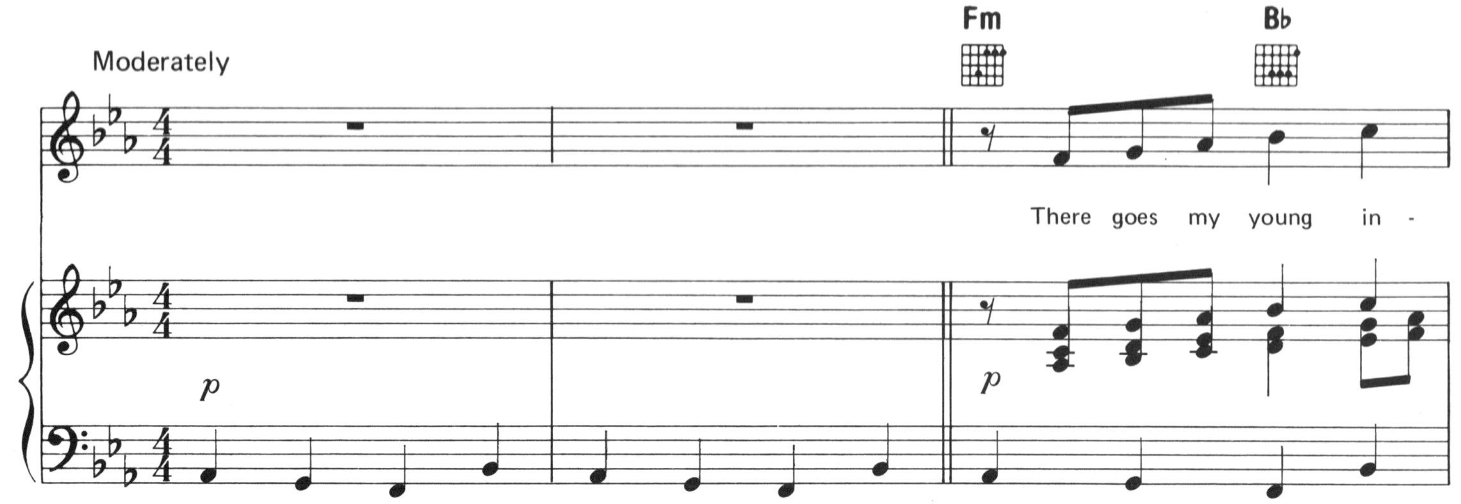

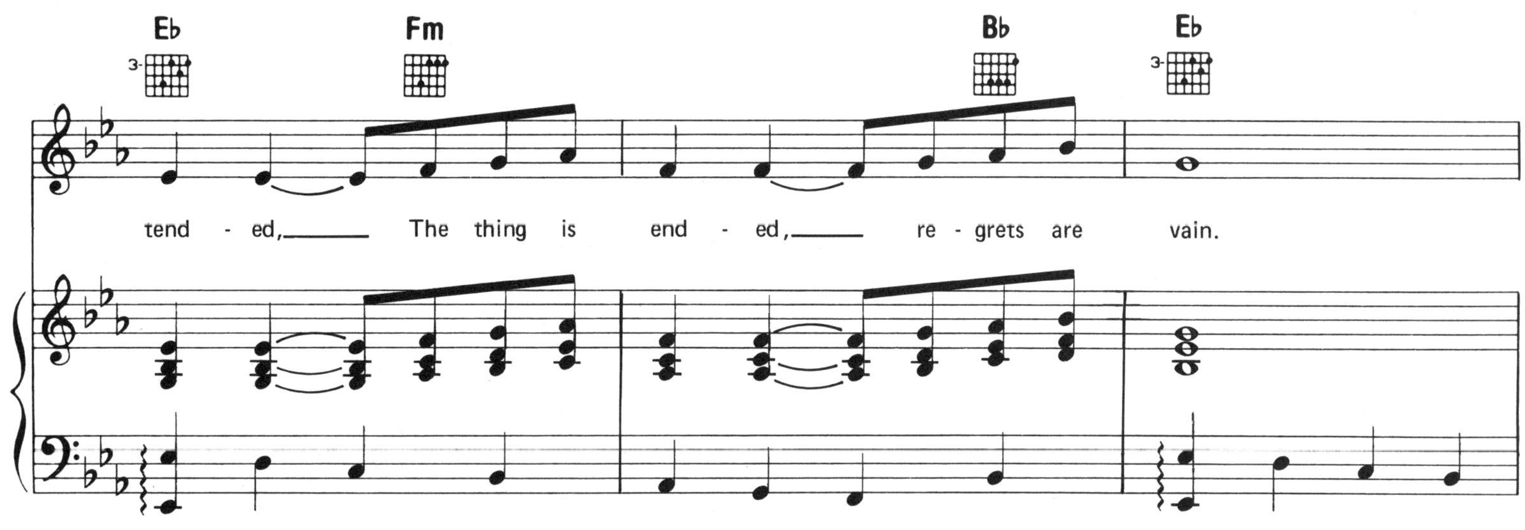

Db
Fm
Bb
Eb
C7
Fm
Cm6
Abmaj7
gain.
I was a good sport,
Told him Good-bye,
Eyes dim,
But why com-
accel.
Slowly with feeling
Bb7
Eb
Fm6
Ab
Gm
Fm
Bb7
plain?
He was too good to me.
How can I get a - long now?
rit.
p - mf
Eb
Fm6
Ab
Gm
Fm
Bb7
Eb
So close he stood to me,
Ev'-ry - thing seems all wrong now!
He would have
Abm
Eb
F7
Bb7
Eb
Ebm6
Bb
F7
brought me the sun.
Mak - ing me smile
That was his

Bb
Ab
Eb
Bb7
Eb
Fm6
Ab
Gm
fun!
When I was mean to him
He'd nev - er say, "Go
Fm
Bb7
Eb
Fm7
Eb
Fm6
Ab
Gm
Fm
Bb7
'way now."
I was a queen to him,
Who's goin' to make me
gay now?
Eb
Abm
Eb
F7
Abm6
Eb
Cm
Fm7
It's on - ly nat - 'ral
I'm blue ooo,
He was too good
Bb9
1 Eb
Cm6
Abmaj7
Bb7
2 Eb
Abmaj7
Eb
to be
true.
true.
rall.
a tempo
cresc.
dim.
Ped.

HERE IN MY ARMS

from DEAREST ENEMY

Words by LORENZ HART
Music by RICHARD RODGERS

Gm7♭5 C7 F B♭ F Dm B♭6 B♭/C C7 F B♭/C C7
5 fr
smile a - way. It's not a mile a - way, but it's new to you.
toll a - way. You'd nev - er stroll a - way, if you on - ly knew!
F Gm7♭5 C7 F6
Here in my arms it's a - dor - a - ble! It's de -
C7 F B♭6 F B♭ F
plor - a - ble that you were nev - er there. When lit - tle
Gm7♭5 C7 F6 C7
lips are so kiss - a - ble it's per - mis - si - ble

F
Bb6
F
Bb
Gb7
for me to ask my share.
Next to my heart it is
Bb
F6
F/E
Dm7
G7
Gm7
3 fr
ev - er so lone - ly, I'm hold - ing on - ly air.
C7#5
F
Gm7b5
5 fr
C7
F
While here in my arms it's a - dor - a - ble! It's de -
C7
F
Bb6
1
F
C7
2
F
plor - a - ble that you were nev - er there.
there.

HELLO, YOUNG LOVERS

from THE KING AND I

Lyrics by OSCAR HAMMERSTEIN II
Music by RICHARD RODGERS

A
D/F#
Fdim7
will.
There are new lov - ers now on the
mf
mp
A7/E
Eb7b5
D
Dm6
same si - lent hill,
Look - ing on the same blue
sea.
And I
A
Dm
know Tom and I are a part of them all,
And they're all a part of Tom
G7
C
C6
Cmaj7
C6
and
me.
Hel -
rit.
mf a tempo

Refrain (very moderately)
C(add9)
C
Cmaj7
C6
lo, young lov - ers, who - ev - er you are, I
p
Cmaj7
C6
G7/B
Fm/C
hope your trou - bles are few
All my good
G7/B
E♭/B♭
6fr
G7/B
Dm7
Dm7/G
G7
wish - es go with you to - night —
I've been in love like
C
C(add9)
C
Cmaj7
you
Be brave, young lov - ers, and fol - low your
mf
p

C6
Cmaj7
C6
G7/B
star, Be brave and faith - ful and true.
Fm/C
G7/B
E♭/B♭
6 fr
G7/B
Dm7
Cling ver - y close to each oth - er to - night —
I've been in
Dm7/G
G7
C
F/A
C7sus/G
3 fr
love like you.
I know how it feels to have
mf
mp
F/A
C7sus/G
3 fr
F/A
C7sus/G
3 fr
C7
F
wings on your heels, And to fly down a street in a trance.

E7
Am
You fly down a street on a chance that you'll meet, And you
Dm7
Dm7/G
G7
meet — not real - ly by chance. Don't
p
C(add9)
C
Cmaj7
C6
Cmaj7
cry, young lov - ers, What - ev - er you do, Don't cry be -
C6
G7/B
Fm/C
G7/B
cause I'm a - lone. All of my mem - 'ries are

E♭/B♭
6fr
G7/B
Dm7
G7
hap - py to - night —
I've had a love of my
C7
F/A
Fm/A♭
own,
I've had a love of my
mf
C+/G
C6/G
Dm
E♭/G
3fr
G7
own, like yours,
I've had a love of my
cresc. ed allargando
1
C6
G7
2
C6
own.
Hel -
own.
mf a tempo
p
f

I COULD WRITE A BOOK

from PAL JOEY

Words by LORENZ HART
Music by RICHARD RODGERS

Gm7
3 fr
C7
Fmaj7
Em7
A7
But my bus - y mind is burn-ing to use what learn-ing I've got.
D7
G/D
G7
Dm7
G7
I won't waste an - y time; I'll strike while the i - ron is hot. If they
C
G7
C
G7
asked me, I could write a book a - bout the
C
G7
C6
C♯dim7
Dm7
G7
G7/F
way you walk and whis - per and look. I could

C/E
A♭7/E♭
Dm7
G7
C
Cdim7
write a pre - face on how we
G/B
C
Cdim7
G/B
E♭7/B♭
Am7
D7
met so the world would nev - er for -
G
Dm7
G7
C
get. And the sim - ple
G7
C
G7
se - cret of the plot is just to

C G7 C6 C♯dim7 Dm7
tell them that I love you a lot.
G7 G7/F C/E A♭7/E♭ Dm7 G7
Then the world dis - cov - ers, as
Gm7 3 fr C7 F Dm7 C/G C+/E F6 G7
my book ends, how to make two lov - ers of
1 C Dm7 G7
friends. If they
2 C F F/C C
friends.

I DIDN'T KNOW WHAT TIME IT WAS

from TOO MANY GIRLS

Words by LORENZ HART
Music by RICHARD RODGERS

E7
A7♭5/E♭
4 fr
D9
4 fr
Am7/G
G/D
Am7/G
G/D
And now I know I was na - ïve!
p
Slowly and tenderly
F♯m7
B7
Bm7/E
Em
F♯m7
B7
I did - n't know what time it was, Then I met
p
A
Am
Em
Bm
you. Oh, what a love - ly time it was,
C
Bm
Am
Dm7
D7
F♯m7
B7
How sub - lime it was, too! I did - n't

Em F♯m7 B7 A Am
know what day it was. You held my hand, Warm like the
Em Bm C Bm Am7 Dm7 D7
month of May it was, And I'll say it was grand.
G Am B7 Am B7
Grand to be a - live, to be young, to be mad, to be yours a -
mf più espressivo
Em C D7 Gmaj7
lone! Grand to see your face, feel your touch, hear your

Em7 A7 Am7 Dm7 D7 F♯m7 B7 Em
voice say I'm all your own! I didn't know what year it was,
p
F♯m7 B7 A Am Em Bm
Life was no prize. I want - ed love and here it was
C Bm Am7 Cm G B7 C6 D7 C6
3 fr
Shin - ing out of your eyes. I'm wise and I know what time it is
1 G Em6 D7
2 G G6
now!
now!
mf
f
8vb

I DO NOT KNOW A DAY I DID NOT LOVE YOU

from TWO BY TWO

Lyrics by MARTIN CHARNIN
Music by RICHARD RODGERS

B♭
F
B♭
C9
F
B♭
B♭maj7
har - vest, when the sun danced in your hair.
I do not know a
cresc.
mf
B♭6
B♭+
B♭
B♭+
B♭6
E
day I did not need you
For shar - ing ev - 'ry mo - ment that I
Am
C9
F
Fmaj7
F6
F+
F
spent.
I need - ed you be - fore I ev - er knew you,
mp
B♭
B♭/A
Gm7
3fr
C7
F6
F
Be - fore I knew what need - ing some - one meant.
And

B♭
B♭/A
Gm7
C9/G
F6/A
F6/C
F/A
Am
B♭
if we ev - er were to have to - mor - row,
as we face the prom - ise of to - mor - row,
One fact a - lone is
mf
E7/B
Am
C7/G
F
Fmaj7
full (and filled with song;)
You will not know a
F6
F+
F
B♭
F/A
day I do not love you
The way that I have loved you
cresc.
Gm7
C9
F
E/F
E♭/F
F
E/F
F
all a - long.
I
long.
f

ISN'T IT ROMANTIC?

from the Paramount Picture LOVE ME TONIGHT

Words by LORENZ HART
Music by RICHARD RODGERS

Eb/G
C7
Fm7
Bb7
kiss just the thing I miss on a night like
mance! I don't give a stitch if I don't get
Eb
Ab
Abm
Eb/G
Gbdim7
this. If dreams are made of i - mag - i - na - tion, I'm not a -
rich. A cus - tom tai - lor who has no cus - tom, is like a
Fm7
Bb7#5
Ebmaj7
fraid of my own cre - a - tion. With all my
sail - or, no one will trust 'em. But there is
Ab
Bb7
Eb/G
Adim
heart, my heart is here for you to take. Why should I
mag - ic in the mu - sic of my shears; I shed no

B♭7
E♭6
F7
B♭7
Steadily, not too fast
E♭
3fr
quake? I'm not a - wake. Is - n't it ro - man - tic?
tears. Lend me your ears! Is - n't it ro - man - tic?
B♭7
E♭
B♭7♯5
E♭
B♭7
Mu - sic in the night, a dream that can be heard. Is - n't it ro -
Soon I will have found some girl that I a - dore. Is - n't it ro -
E♭
B♭7
E♭
man - tic? Mov - ing shad - ows write the old - est mag - ic
man - tic? While I sit a - round, my love can scrub the
C7♯5
C7
Fm
C7
Fm
B♭7
G7
word. I hear the breez - es play - ing
floor. She'll kiss me ev - 'ry hour,

Cm G7#5 Cm Eb7/Bb Ab C7/G
3 fr
3 fr
4 fr
in the trees a - bove. While
or she'll get the sack. And
Fm Bb7 Bdim7 Cm F9 Bbdim7 Bb7
3 fr
all the world is say - ing you were meant for love. Is - n't it ro -
when I take a show - er she can scrub my back. Is - n't it ro -
Eb Bb7 Eb Bb7#5
3 fr
3 fr
man - tic? Mere - ly to be young on such a night as
man - tic? On a moon-light night she'll cook me on - ion
Eb Bb7 Eb Bb7
3 fr
3 fr
this? Is - n't it ro - man - tic? Ev - 'ry note that's sung is
soup. Kid - dies are ro - man - tic, and if we don't fight, we

Eb
C7#5
C7
Fm
C7
Fm
like a lov - er's kiss. Sweet
soon will have a troupe! We'll
Bb7
G7
Cm
Cm/Bb
Cm/A
Abm6
sym-bols in the moon-light, do you mean that I will fall in
help the pop-u-la-tion, it's a du - ty that we owe to
Eb/G
Edim7
Bb7
1
Eb
Gbdim7
love per - chance? Is - n't it ro - mance?
dear old France. Is - n't it ro -
Bb7
2
Eb
Abm6
Eb6
Is - n't it ro - mance?

I HAVE DREAMED
from THE KING AND I

Lyrics by OSCAR HAMMERSTEIN II
Music by RICHARD RODGERS

B♭7
E♭
3fr
time and a - gain, I've thought all the things that
F7
B♭7
you were think - ing too.
E♭6
B♭7
E♭6
I have dreamed that your arms are love - ly
B♭9
I have dreamed what a joy you'll be

F6
C7
F6
I have dreamed ev-'ry word you'll whis - per
Bb9
Eb6
Cm7
3fr
F7
Bb
when you're close, close to me.
D7
G
Gmaj7
G6
How you look in the glow of eve - ning
G
Gmaj7
I have dreamed and en-joyed the
3
3

B♭9
A♭/B♭
B♭7
E♭/G
G7
view
In these dreams I've loved you so that by
Cm
F7
E♭/B♭
A♭
G7
now I think I know what it's like to be loved by
Cm
F9♯11
F9
B♭6
Adim7
B♭9sus
B♭7
you
I will love be - ing loved by
1
E♭
B♭7
you.
2
E♭
you.

IF I LOVED YOU

from CAROUSEL

Lyrics by OSCAR HAMMERSTEIN II
Music by RICHARD RODGERS

Allegretto moderato

N.C.

mp

A7 D

p

When I worked in the mill, Weav-in' at the loom, I'd gaze ab-sent -
Kind - a scraw - ny and pale, Pick-in' at my food And love - sick like

Db

mind - ed at the roof ___ And half the time the shut - tle 'd
an - y oth - er guy ___ I'd throw a - way my sweat - er and

tan - gle in the threads, And the warp 'd get mixed with the woof ___
dress up like a dude in a dick - ey and a col - lar and a tie ___

A
If I loved you!
If I loved you!
Oh,
Oh,
D/F♯
C(add9)/G
C/G
G7
some - how I can see just ex - ack - ly how I'd be.
p
rit.
Refrain (with great warmth and slowly)
C
Cdim7
C/E
E+
If I loved you, Time and a - gain I would try to say
mf
Dm/F
D♯dim7
C/E
Em
All I'd want you to know.
cross hands

C
Cdim7
C/E
If I loved you,
Words wouldn't come in an
E+
Dm/F
D♯dim7
C/E
eas - y way, 'Round in cir - cles I'd go.
cresc.
E+
Am
Dm
C♯7
Long - in' to tell you, but a - fraid and
mf espr.
C/G
Dm/F
B♭
D/A
shy, I'd let my gold - en chanc - es pass me

G
G7
Cdim7
C/E
by! Soon you'd leave me, off you would go in the
E+
Dm/F
D♯dim7
C/G
Em
mist of day, Nev - er, nev - er to know
C
Em
Dm/F
C/E
Dm7
Dm7/G
G7
How I loved you, If I
mf molto espr.
f
rit.
1 C
Dm7/G
G7
2 C
loved you.
loved you.
a tempo
L.H.

LOVE, LOOK AWAY

from FLOWER DRUM SONG

Lyrics by OSCAR HAMMERSTEIN II
Music by RICHARD RODGERS

D♯dim7
Cmaj7
F6
sea. Call it a day. Love, let us say we're
C(add9)
C
Bdim7
E7♭9
Am
F6
G7sus
through. No good are you for me, No good am I for
C
F6
F6/E
Dm7
G7
C
you. Want - ing you so, I try too much.
mf
espressivo
F6
F6/E
Dm7
G7
Cmaj7
Af - ter you go, I cry too much.
mf

G7
Cmaj7
Love, look a - way.
p
F6
C(add9)
C
Bdim7
E7♭9
Lone - ly though I may be,
Leave me and set me
cresc.
Am
Dm7♭5
Cmaj7/G
Dm7
G7
free,
Look a - way, look a-way, look a - way from
f molto espr.
1 C
F
G7
2 C
Fmaj7
Dm7
C
me.
me.
mp
rall.
mp
p
Ped.
*

LOVER

from the Paramount Picture LOVE ME TONIGHT

Words by LORENZ HART
Music by RICHARD RODGERS

D
D6
Em7
A7
D
Since you took con - trol of my life you have be -
C♯7
F♯m
Bm
Em7
come the whole of my life. When you are a - way it's
A7
F♯m
D6
E7
A7
aw - ful and when you are with me it's worse.
D
G♯m7
4 fr
C♯7
Gm7
3 fr
Lov - er, when I'm near you and I hear you

C7
F♯m7
B7
Fm7
B♭7
speak my name
soft - ly in my
Em7
A7
D
D7
G
ear you breathe a flame.
A7
D
G♯m7
4 fr
C♯7
Lov - er, when we're danc - ing, keep on
Lov - er, it's im - mor - al, but why
Gm7
3 fr
C7
F♯m7
B7
Fm7
glanc - ing in my eyes till love's
quar - rel with our bliss when two

B♭7
Em7
A7
D
own entranc - ing music dies.
lips of cor - al want to kiss?
F♯
G♯m7
4 fr
All of my fu - ture is in you.
I say "The Dev - il is in you,"
C♯7
F♯
G♯m7
4 fr
C♯7
Your ev - 'ry plan I de - sign.
and to re - sist you I try;
A
Bm7
2 fr
E7
Em7/A
Prom - ise you'll al - ways con - tin - ue to be mine.
but if you did - n't con - tin - ue I would die!

A7
D
G♯m7
C♯7
4fr
Lov - er, please be ten - der. When you're
Gm7
3fr
C7
F♯m7
B7
Fm7
ten - der, fears de - part.
Lov - er,
B♭7
Em7
A7
1
D6
Bm
I sur - ren - der to my heart.
Em7
A7
2
D6
Bm
Em7
A7
D
heart.
8va basso

THE MOST BEAUTIFUL GIRL IN THE WORLD

from JUMBO

Words by LORENZ HART
Music by RICHARD RODGERS

Dm7
G7
G+
3 fr
C
Dm7
G7
We used to laugh and sing to - geth - er be - fore we
p
C
G7
learned how to talk.
mf
C
E
F
G7
B
C
With no rea - son for the sea - son
p
Am7
D7
Dm7
G7
Spring would end as it would start.
mf

C/E
E/F
F
G7
Now the sea - son has a
p
B/C
C
Am7
D7
G
rea - son, And there's spring - time in my heart.
cresc.
B♭m6/D♭
3 fr
C
f
C7
Fmaj7
Fdim7
The most beau - ti - ful girl in the world Picks my
p

Fmaj7
Fdim7/C
Fmaj7
Fdim7/C
C7sus/G
3 fr
C7
ties out, eats my can - dy, Drinks my bran - dy, The most
F/A
Am/C
Gm7
3 fr
C7
beau - ti - ful girl in the world. The most
mf
Fmaj7
Fdim7
Fmaj7
Fdim7/C
beau - ti - ful star in the world is - n't Gar - bo, Is - n't
Fmaj7
Fdim7/C
C7sus/G
3 fr
C7
Diet - rich But the sweet trick who can make me be - lieve it's a
cresc.

Cm/E♭
Cm
Am7♭5
D7
Dm
G9
beau - ti - ful world.
So - cial not a
mf
C7
Dm
G9
C7
bit,
Nat - 'ral kind of wit,
Am7
D7
G7sus/D
G7
Gm7
C
She'd shine an - y - where
And she has - n't got plat - i - num
Gm
C7
Fmaj7
Fdim7
hair
The most beau - ti - ful house in the world
Has a
p

Fmaj7
Fdim7/C
Fmaj7
Fdim7/C
C7sus/G
3 fr
C7
mort - gage what do I care, it's good-bye care when my
Cm/E♭
3 fr
Cm
3 fr
Am7♭5
D7
slip - pers are next to the ones that be - long
To the
cresc.
Dm7
G7
Gm7
3 fr
B♭7
1
F
B♭
one and on - ly beau - ti - ful girl in the world!
f
F
C7
2
F
B♭
F
The most world!
mf
f

MY FUNNY VALENTINE

from BABES IN ARMS

Words by LORENZ HART
Music by RICHARD RODGERS

G
Cm
3 fr
Fm
made, Thy va - cant brow and thy tous - led hair con -
Eb
3 fr
Cm
3 fr
ceal thy good in - tent. Thou no - ble, up - right,
Bb7
Cm
3 fr
G7
G7#5
truth - ful, sin - cere and slight - ly dop - ey gent, you're
Cm
3 fr
Cm(maj7)
3 fr
Cm7
3 fr
My fun - ny Val - en - tine, Sweet com - ic
p

Cm6
Fm/C
Fm
Val - en - tine, You make me smile with my
Dm7♭5
G7
Fm/A♭
G7
heart.
Cm
Cm(maj7)
Cm7
3 fr
Your looks are laugh - a - ble, Un - pho - to -
F7/C
Fm/C
Fm7
graph - a - ble, yet you're my fav - 'rite work of

A♭m/C♭
A♭m/F
B♭7
B♭/A♭
E♭/G
B♭7
art.
Is your fig - ure less than
mf
E♭/G
B♭7
E♭6/G
B♭7
E♭/G
B♭7
Greek; Is your mouth a lit - tle weak, when you
E♭maj7/G
G7
Cm
A♭maj7
A♭6
o - pen it to speak, Are you smart?
A♭7
G7
Cm
Cm(maj7)
But don't change a hair for me,
p

Cm7
F7/C
Fm7/C
Not if you care for me, Stay, lit - tle
poco a poco cresc.
D7♭5/A♭
G7
Cm
E♭7
Val - en - tine, stay!
f molto espress.
A♭
A♭maj7/G
Fm7
B♭7
1
E♭
Each day is Val - en - tine's day.
mf
A♭7
G7
2
E♭
E♭6
day.
8vb

PEOPLE WILL SAY WE'RE IN LOVE

from OKLAHOMA!

Lyrics by OSCAR HAMMERSTEIN II
Music by RICHARD RODGERS

Em
A7
Dm
D7
prove what they say is quite un - true.
carved our i - ni - tials on the tree!
G
Gm
3 fr
D
D7/C
Here is the gist, a prac - ti - cal list of "dont's" for
Jist keep a slice of all the ad - vice you give so
G/B
G7
C
you. Don't throw bou -
free. Don't praise my
mf
quets at me. Don't please
charm too much. Don't look

G7
my folks too much.
so vain with me.
C
D9
4fr
Don't laugh at my jokes too much.
Don't stand in the rain with me.
Dm7
G7♭9
4fr
C
Peo - ple will say we're in love!
Peo - ple will say we're in love!
C♯dim7
G7
C
Don't sigh and gaze at me.
Don't take my arm too much.

G7
Your sighs are so like mine.
Don't keep your hand in mine.
C
Your eyes must - n't glow like mine.
Your hand feels so grand in mine.
D9
4 fr
Dm7
G7
Peo - ple will say we're in love!
Peo - ple will say we're in love!
C
Cm7
3 fr
F7
F7♭9
Don't start col -
Don't dance all

B♭+ B♭ Bm7♭5 E7 A7♭9 A7
lect - ing things. Give me my rose and my
night with me. Till the stars fade from a -
D7 Dm7 Cdim7 C
glove. Sweet - heart they're sus -
bove. They'll see it's al -
Am7 D7 C G+ C Dm/G D♭/G G7
3fr
pect - ing things. Peo - ple will say we're in
right with me. Peo - ple will say we're in
1 C Am Dm7 Dm7/G
love.
2 C C(add9)
love.

MY HEART STOOD STILL

from A CONNECTICUT YANKEE

Words by LORENZ HART
Music by RICHARD RODGERS

A
Bm7/E
E7
C
Ice - land Was my heart's do - main. I
Pla - to, Love, I thought a sin; But
G7
C
C/B♭
Am7
A♭dim7
4fr
saw your eyes; Now cas - tles rise in Spain!
since your kiss, I'm read - ing Mis - sus Glyn!
Gm7/C
C7
F
G♯dim7
Gm7
3fr
C7
I took one look at you,
rit.
F
F+
Gm7
3fr
C7
F
F+
That's all I meant to do; And then my

B♭6 C7 F Gm7 C7 F G♯dim7
3 fr
heart stood still! My feet could
Gm7 C7 F F+ Gm7 C7
3 fr
3 fr
step and walk, My lips could move and talk,
F F+ B♭6 C7 F B♭6 F
And yet my heart stood still! Though not a
Fm C+ C
sin - gle word was spok - en, I could tell you knew, That un - felt

Dm7♭5
G7
C7
clasp of hands Told me so well you knew.
rall.
F
G♯dim7
Gm7
3 fr
C7
F
F+
I nev - er lived at all Un - til the
a tempo
B♭
Gm7
3 fr
F/C
C7
thrill of that mo - ment when My heart stood
1
F
Dm6
Am
C7
still.
2
F
still.

MY ROMANCE

from JUMBO

Words by LORENZ HART
Music by RICHARD RODGERS

C#m7♭5
D7
G7
Dm7
G7sus
G7
flow - 'ry fuss, no sir, ma - dam, not for us. My ro -
C
G/B
Am
C/G
F
F/A
mance does - n't have to have a moon in the
C
Am
G6
F
C/E
sky. My ro - mance does - n't need a blue la -
Dm
G7sus
G7
C
F
goon stand - ing by. No month of

C(add9)
C9
F
C(add9)
May, no twink - ling stars, no
F♯m7
B7
Em
Am7
G/D
D7
hide a - way, no soft gui -
G7sus
G7
C
G/B
Am
C/G
tars. My ro - mance does - n't need a cas - tle
F
F/A
C
Am
G6
ris - ing in Spain nor a dance to a

F
C/E
Dm
G7sus
G7
C
C9
con - stant - ly sur - pris - ing re - frain. Wide a -
F
A7
Dm
E7
A7
wake I can make my most fan - tas - tic dreams come
D7
C/G
Am
Dm7
G9
true. My ro - mance does - n't need a thing but
1 C
D7
G9
2 C
C6/9
you. My ro - you.

NO OTHER LOVE

from ME AND JULIET

Lyrics by OSCAR HAMMERSTEIN II
Music by RICHARD RODGERS

Ab7
4fr
G7b5
Gb7
F7b5
How man - y moons to see, dear, Till you come back to me, dear?
Bb7
G7
C7sus
C7
F
When will I know? When will I know?
sf
rit.
a tempo
Refrain (slow Tango tempo)
F
No oth - er love have I
On - ly my love for you
mp
E
Gm/Bb
G/B
On - ly the dream we knew

Gb7b5
Fmaj7
F
No oth - er love.
Watch-ing the night go by
E
Wish - ing that you could be
Gm/Bb
G/B
Gb7b5
Watch - ing the night with me
In - to the night I
F
Eb
3 fr
Bb7
C/E
cry, hur-ry home, come home to me.
Set me
mf

G7/D
A/C#
D
G
free, free from doubt and free
C7
F
from long - ing. In - to your arms I'll fly
Locked in your arms I'll stay
sf
mf
p
E
Gm/Bb
G/B
Gb7b5
Wait - ing to hear you say
No oth - er love have
F
Bb
Gm7
F
C9sus
C7
F
I, No oth - er love.
f
rit.

SOME ENCHANTED EVENING

from SOUTH PACIFIC

Lyrics by OSCAR HAMMERSTEIN II
Music by RICHARD RODGERS

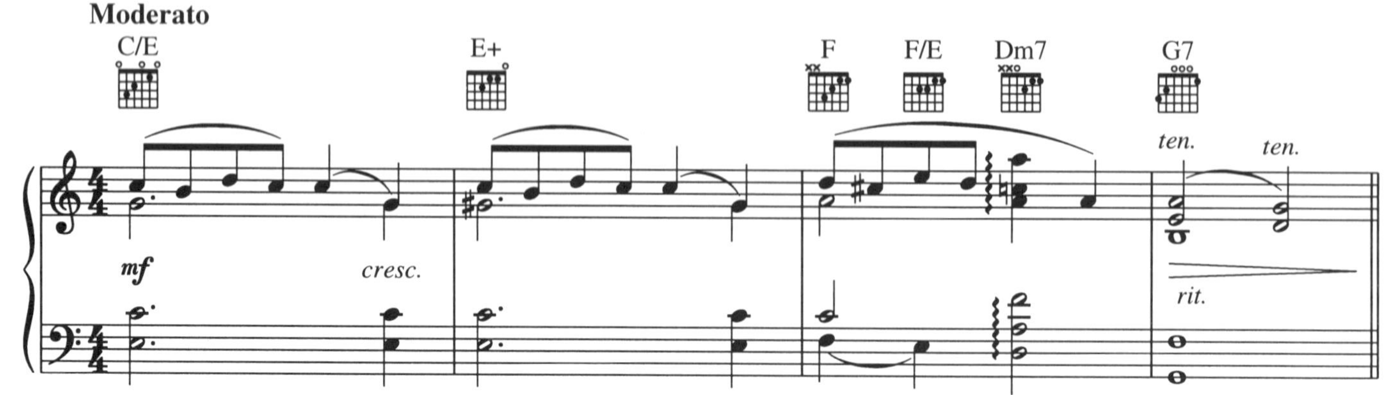

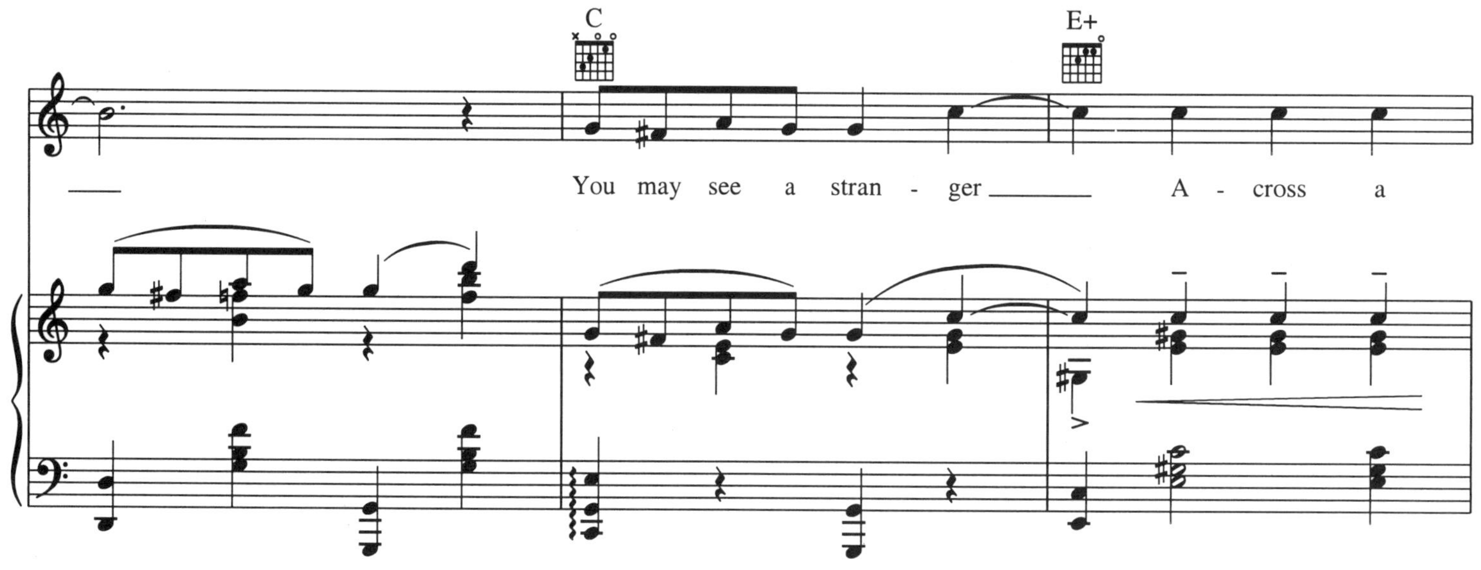

Fmaj7
F6
C6/E
Dm7
G7
Dm
E7
crowd - ed room And some-how you know, You know e - ven
Am
C7/G
F
C/E
Dm7
G7
then That some-where you'll see her a - gain and a -
mf
Cmaj7
C7
C+
Cdim7/G
C
gain. Some en - chant - ed eve - ning
p
G7
Some-one may be laugh - ing,

C
E+
Fmaj7
F6
You may hear her laugh - ing A - cross a crowd - ed room
C6/E
Dm7
G7
Dm
E7
Am
C7/G
And night af - ter night, As strange as it seems,
F
C/E
Dm7
G7
C
The sound of her laugh - ter will sing in your dreams.
mf
G7sus
G7
Cmaj9
C
Dm7
G7
C6
C
Who can ex - plain it? Who can tell you why?
pp
tenderly and legato

G7sus G7 Cmaj9 C Am7 D7 G Cm6
Fools give you reas - ons, Wise men nev - er try.
cresc. molto
Edim7 Dm7/G Cdim7/G C
Some en - chant - ed eve - ning
mp
Dm7 G7 C
When you find your true love,
When you feel her call you
E+ Fmaj7 F6 C6/E
A - cross a crowd - ed room,
Then fly to her
mf

Dm7
G7
Dm7
E7
Am
C7/G
F
C/E
side
And make her your own,
Or all through your
f
molto espr.
Dm
Dm7/G
G7
C
life you may dream all a - lone.
rit.
a tempo
dim.
G7sus
G7
Cmaj9
C
Dm7
G7
C6
C
G7sus
G7
Cmaj9
C
Once you have found her, Nev - er let her go. Once you have found her,
pp legatissimo
Dm7/G
C
Nev - er let her go!
rit.
mf

SOMETHING GOOD

from THE SOUND OF MUSIC

Lyrics and Music by
RICHARD RODGERS

F/C
C7
F6
F7
must have been a mo - ment of truth.
For
Bb/D
Db7
F/C
F
here you are, Stand - ing there, Lov - ing me,
mf
Bb/D
Db7
C9
C7
Wheth - er or not you should.
So,
mp
F
F7
Bb
Gm7b5
F/C
some-where in my youth or child - hood
I must have done

1.
2.
E/C
C7
F
Gm7/C
C7
F
some - thing
good.
Per -
good.
mf
Coda
C7/B♭
Am7
F/A
Gm7
Gm7♭5
Noth - ing comes from noth - ing,
Noth - ing ev - er could.
So,
mf
F/C
B♭/C
C7
some - where in my youth
or child - hood
I
F/C
E/C
C7
F
must have done
some - thing
good.
mf

SOMETHING WONDERFUL

from THE KING AND I

Lyrics by OSCAR HAMMERSTEIN II
Music by RICHARD RODGERS

A13/D
5 fr
F♯/D
give and for - give and help and pro - tect, as long as you
Moderato
G
F♯/G
C
live.
mf
dim.
Refrain (slowly, with expression)
D+
He will not al - ways say What you would have him say,
p
C/E
Am7
D7
But, now and then, he'll say some - thing won - der - ful.

G
D+
C
G
D+
C
The thought-less things he'll do will hurt and wor - ry you
G
C/E
A7
D
Then, all at once, he'll do some-thing won - der - ful. He
Gm
Dm/F
Gm
A7
D
has a thou - sand dreams that won't come true. You
più espressivo
Gm
Gm/F
A7/E
D
know that he be - lieves in them And that's e - nough for you.
cresc.
mf

G
D+
C
G
D+
C
G
You'll al - ways go a - long, De - fend him when he's wrong And tell him
p
C/E
A7
D/F♯
B7
Em
when he's strong, He is won - der - ful. He'll al - ways need your love
mf
G7
C/E
G/D
D+
C/D
G/D
And so he'll get your love A man who needs your love can be
dim.
p
C/D
1
G
F♯/G
C/G
2
G
won - der - ful.
mf
dim.
pp

THE SWEETEST SOUNDS

from NO STRINGS

Lyrics and Music by
RICHARD RODGERS

E7
A7
Dm
hear Are still in- side my head.
The kind- est words I'll ev- er
Gm
Gm7
C7
Fmaj7
F6
know Are wait- ing to be said.
Gm6
A7
Dm
Gm
The most en- tranc- ing sight of
E7
A7
Cm7
all is yet for me to see.

F7
Bb
G7
Bdim
F6
And the dear- est love in all the
F
Gm7
C7
Fmaj7
world Is wait- ing some- where for me.
F7
Bb6
Gm7
C7
Is wait- ing some- where, Some- where for
1.
F
Fmaj7
Gm
A7
me.
The
mf
mp
2.
F
Gb6
F6
me.
mf
f
sf

THERE'S A SMALL HOTEL

from ON YOUR TOES

Words by LORENZ HART
Music by RICHARD RODGERS

Am7
D7
Gmaj7
G6
plete for us to share to - geth - er.
Gmaj7
G6
C
Dm7
G7
Look - ing through the win - dow you can
mf
C
D♯dim
E7
Am
see a dis - tant stee - ple; Not a sign of
E7
F
Am
Cm7
D7
Gmaj7
G6
peo - ple, Who wants peo - ple? When the
3fr
p

Gmaj7
G6
G
steele - ple bell says, "Good - night, sleep well," we'll
Am7
1
D7
Gmaj7
G6
Am7
D7
thank the small ho - tel to - geth - er.
2
D7
B♭
Cm7
3 fr
F7
tel. We'll creep in - to our lit - tle shell And we will
G
Am7
D7
Gmaj7
thank the small ho - tel to - geth - er.
rit.
L.H.
mf
Ped.

TEN MINUTES AGO
from CINDERELLA

Lyrics by OSCAR HAMMERSTEIN II
Music by RICHARD RODGERS

Em
Cm6
G/D
A9
Am7/D
gave me the feel - ing the room had no ceil - ing or floor.
D7
G
D7sus/A
D7
G
Ten min - utes a - go, I met you, And we mur - mured our
D7sus/A
D7
G
B7
how - do - you - do's, I want - ed to ring out the
Em
Cm6
G/D
D7
G
F/G
G7
bells and fling out my arms and to sing out the news. I have

C
C/G
F♯m7♭5/G
3fr
G/B
G/D
Am7
found her! She's an an - gel with the dust of the
sf
D7
G(add9)
G
F/G
G7
C
C/G
F♯m7♭5/G
3fr
G/B
stars in her eyes. We are danc - ing, we are fly - ing
sf
G/D
A9/E
A
G
A7
Am7/D
D7
And she's tak - ing me back to the skies. In the
f
mp
G
D7sus/A
D7
G
arms of my love, I'm fly - ing o - ver moun - tain and mead - ow and

D7sus/A D7 G B7 Em
glen And I like it so well, that for all I can
Cm6 G/D D7 Dm7 G7 C
tell, I may nev - er come down a - gain! I may nev - er come
Am7 Am7/D D7 1 G Em7
down to earth a - gain.
Am7 D7 2 G A7♭5(♭9) D7 G
Ten gain.
f
sf
mp

THIS CAN'T BE LOVE

from THE BOYS FROM SYRACUSE

Words by LORENZ HART
Music by RICHARD RODGERS

Smoothly
G/D
C♯dim7/D
Am/D
D7
G6
Poor half - wit!
This can't be
poco rit.
p a tempo
C7
C13
G
love be - cause I feel so well,
No sobs, no sor -
G6
Am7
D7
Am7
D7
G6
- rows, no sighs;
This can't be love, I get no
mf
p
C7
C13
G/D
A7♭9
Am9
D7
diz - zy spell.
My head is not in the

G
C6
C7
G/B
F♯m7
B7
Em
skies. My heart does not stand still, Just hear it beat!
mf
B7♯9
E7♯5(♭9)
A9
D7♭9
4 fr
D7
This is too sweet to be love.
G6
C7
C13
2 fr
G6/D
3 fr
C♯dim7/D
Am7
This can't be love be-cause I feel so well, But still I love to look in your eyes.
p
1
G
Am7
D7
2
G
C7/B♭
Am7
Am7/D
G
eyes.
mf
mf

WE KISS IN A SHADOW
from THE KING AND I

Lyrics by OSCAR HAMMERSTEIN II
Music by RICHARD RODGERS

C7
whis - per, A - fraid to be heard; When peo - ple are
F
Am
near, we speak not a word. A - lone in our
mp
B7
Em
C
F
se - cret, To - geth - er we sigh For one smil - ing
cresc.
E
D7
E7
Am
C7
F
day to be free To kiss in the
mf
p
legato

C7
sun - light
And say to the sky
F7
F7+5
Be - hold and be - lieve what you see!
Be -
Bbmaj7
Dm
Gm7
C9
F
hold how my lov - er loves me!
mf
F
me!
mp
p
morendo
pp
Ped.

WAIT TILL YOU SEE HER

from BY JUPITER

Words by LORENZ HART
Music by RICHARD RODGERS

Eb
Bb7
Eb
Bb7
That's not my light - heart - ed friend!"
Meet - ing one
Bb+/Eb
Eb
Bb+
Eb
Bb+
Eb
Bb7
girl was the start of the end.
Love is a
Bb+/Eb
Eb
Bb+
Eb
Bb+
Eb
F7
Bb7
sim - ple e - mo - tion a friend should com - pre -
Eb
Ebm
Eb
Eb+
hend.
poco a poco cresc.

Spirited
Fm7
Fm7/B♭
B♭7
E♭
3 fr
Wait till you see her, see how she looks, Wait till you
mp
Fm7/B♭
B♭9
Emaj7
E♭6
hear her laugh.
Paint - ers of paint - ings,
Fm7
D7
Gm
writ - ers of books, Nev - er could tell the half.
Cm
Cm7/F
F7
B♭
Wait till you feel the warmth of her glance,
mf

Cm7
G7#5(b9)
C9b5
C9
Fm7
Bb7
Pen - sive and sweet and wise. All of it love - ly,
mp
Cm
Gm
C9
F9
Fm/Ab
G7
All of it thrill - ing; I'll nev - er be will - ing to free her,
cresc.
f
Ebm/Gb
F7
E7
Eb7
Fm7/Ab
Bb7
When you see her, You won't be - lieve your
rit.
1
Eb
eyes.
a tempo
2
Eb
Eb6
eyes.
rall.
f

WHEN THE CHILDREN ARE ASLEEP

from CAROUSEL

Lyrics by OSCAR HAMMERSTEIN II
Music by RICHARD RODGERS

Eb/C
3 fr
Am7
D7
G
sit - tin' room, where we love to be by our - selves, Where the
Bb9
Eb6
Fm7/Bb
Bb7
flick - rin' glow of the fi - re - light makes the books wink down from their
tr
tr
Eb(add9)
Eb
Bb7sus
Bb7
Gm7/Bb
Eb/Bb
shelves. And there ev - 'ry eve - nin', we'll al - ways be,
Ebdim7/Bb
Bb9/F
Gm/Bb
Gbdim7
Bb7/F
Bb7
Me in my arm - chair, You on my knee.

Refrain
Eb
Fm7
Fm7/Bb
Bb7
Eb
When the chil - dren are a - sleep, we'll sit and dream
p - mf
Ab6
G7
Cm7
F7
The things that ev - 'ry oth - er dad and moth - er
Bb9
Gm/Bb
Ebdim/Bb
Bb7
Eb
Fm7
Fm7/Bb
Bb7
dream.
When the chil - dren are a - sleep and lights are
C
Cmaj7
C6
Ab/G
Fmaj7/G
Bb7
Eb
low,
If I still love you the way I

Bb7
G7
Cm
Fm
G7
G7#5
Cm
Cm/Bb
love you to - day, You'll par - don my say - ing
F7/A Cm7/G
F7
Bb7
Eb
Fm7
Fm7/Bb Bb7
"I told you so!" When the chil-dren are a - sleep, I'll dream with
mf - p
G7#5
G7
C7b9
Dbm/Ab A/G
Fm7
Eb/G
Fm7/Ab
Bb7
you We'll think what fun we have had and be glad that it all came
1 Eb
Bb9
2 Eb
Ab6
Eb
true!
true!
mf
f

WHERE OR WHEN

from BABES IN ARMS

Words by LORENZ HART
Music by RICHARD RODGERS

Ab
4fr
Fm7
Fm7b5
Fm7/Bb
Bb7
Eb
3fr
Things you do come back to you, As though they knew the way. Oh, the
Fm
Bb7
Eb
3fr
Eb6
tricks your mind can play! It seems we stood and talked like
poco. rit.
a tempo
Ebmaj7
3fr
Fm7
this be - fore. We looked at each oth - er in the same way then,
Ebmaj7
3fr
Eb6
Fm7b5
Bb7
But I can't re-mem - ber where or when.

Eb
Eb6
Ebmaj7
3 fr
The clothes you're wear - ing are the clothes you wore. The
Fm7
smile you are smil-ing you were smil - ing then, But I can't re-mem - ber where or
Ebmaj7
Eb6
Dm7b5
G7
Cm
Fm7
when. Some things that hap - pen for the
G7sus
G7
F/G
G7
Cm
Fm7
first time, Seem to be hap - pen - ing a -

Cm7
F7
Fm7/B♭
B♭7
E♭
E♭6
gain.
And so it seems that we have
E♭maj7
G+
A♭6
B♭6
met be - fore, and laughed be - fore, and
A♭6
Gm
Fm
B♭7
loved be - fore, But who knows where or
1
E♭
Fm/E♭
E♭maj7
Fm/E♭
B♭7sus
B♭7
2
E♭
A♭m7
E♭
when!
when!
rit.
L.H.

WITH A SONG IN MY HEART

from SPRING IS HERE

Words by LORENZ HART
Music by RICHARD RODGERS

Bbm7
Eb7
Ab
4 fr
B
time
light
Ev - 'ry meet - ing's a mar - vel - ous pas - time You're in -
Not a note of our mu - sic is played out, It will
Eb/Bb
6 fr
Cm
3 fr
Fm7
Bb7
Eb
3 fr
Ab
4 fr
creas - ing - ly sweet, So when - ev - er we hap - pen to meet
be just as sweet, And an air that I'll live to re - peat:
Eb
3 fr
E7/B
Bb7
Bb7#5(b9)
Eb
3 fr
Bb7
I greet you With a song in my heart.
rall.
a tempo
Eb
3 fr
Bb7
Eb
3 fr
G7
I be-hold your a - dor - a - ble face, Just a song at the start,
R.H.

Cm
G7
Cm
Cm/B♭
But it soon is a hymn to your grace. When the mu - sic
Am7♭5
A♭
Fm7
E♭6
D7
swells I'm touch-ing your hand; It tells that you're
cresc.
Fm
D7
G7
C7
Fm
B♭7
E♭
stand - ing near, and At the sound of your
dim.
p
B♭7
E♭
B♭7
voice Heav-en o - pens its por - tals to me.

Eb
G7
Cm
Can I help but re - joice
That a song such as
ours came to be?
But I al - ways knew
I would live life
through
With a song in my heart
for
you.
you.
Cm/Bb
Am7b5
F7
Eb/Bb
Ab6
Bb7
E7/B
Bb7#5(b9)
3 fr
6 fr
mp
cresc.
rall.
a tempo
p
1
2

YOU ARE NEVER AWAY

from ALLEGRO

Lyrics by OSCAR HAMMERSTEIN II
Music by RICHARD RODGERS

G6
Gmaj7
G6
Am7
D7
day when you don't play a part
Am7
D7
Gmaj7
G6
Gmaj7
In a word that I say
G6
E7/B
Am
Am7
Am7♭5
Or a sight that I see.
Cm6
G/D
Em
Am
Am7
You are nev - er a - way and I'll nev - er

D7
E♭6
be free.
You're the
E♭
smile on my face, or a song that I sing; You're a
B♭9/E♭
rain - bow I chase on a morn - ing in Spring; You're a
E♭
star in the lace of a wild wil - low tree, In the

G/D
Gdim7/D
3 fr
Am7
Am7/D
D7
green leaf - y lace of a wild wil - low
G
Gdim7
G
tree. But to - night you're no
mf
mp
G6
Gmaj7
G6
Bdim
F7
star, Nor a song that I sing
G
G6
Gmaj7
In my arms where you are, you are sweet - er

G6
Am7
D7
Am7
D7
than Spring; In my
mf
Gmaj7
G6
Gmaj7
G6
E7/B
Am
arms where you are Cling-ing close-ly to
Am7
Am7♭5
Cm6
G/D
me You are love-li-er by
Em
F♯m7♭5
4 fr
Am/B
B7
Em
far, than I dreamed you could be

A9
G/D
Gdim7/D
3 fr
You are love - li - er, my
mf rit.
accel.
Am7
D9
4 fr
dar - ling, than I dreamed you
opt.
rit.
G
Gdim7
ten.
could be!
8va
poco rit.
f a tempo
Cdim7/G

YOU'RE NEARER

from TOO MANY GIRLS

Words by LORENZ HART
Music by RICHARD RODGERS

Dm/C
C♯dim
Dm7
nev - er far a - way from me, For you're too much my own.
G7-9
C
Cmaj7
C6
Dm7
G7
You're near - er than my head is to my pil - low,
p mf
Dm7
G7
C
Cmaj7
C6
Near - er than the wind is
Dm7
G7
Dm7
G7
C
to the wil - low,
Dear - er
mf

D7
G7
E7
Am
Am7
than the rain is to the earth be - low,
f
D7
Gmaj7
C
F
Fmaj7
Prec - ious as the sun to the things that grow.
mp
mf
Dm7
G7-9
C
Cmaj7
C6
You're near - er than the i - vy
p
Dm7
G7
Dm7
G7
C
to the wall is, Near - er
mf

D7
G7
E7
Bm7
E7
than the win - ter
to the fall
is,
mf
Am
Am7
D7
C
Leave
me,
but when you're
a - way
You'll
Abm6
C
Em
Dm7
G7
know
You're
near - er
for I love you
1 C
G7-9
2 C
so.
You're
so.
f
mf
rall.
3
p

YOUNGER THAN SPRINGTIME

from SOUTH PACIFIC

Lyrics by OSCAR HAMMERSTEIN II
Music by RICHARD RODGERS

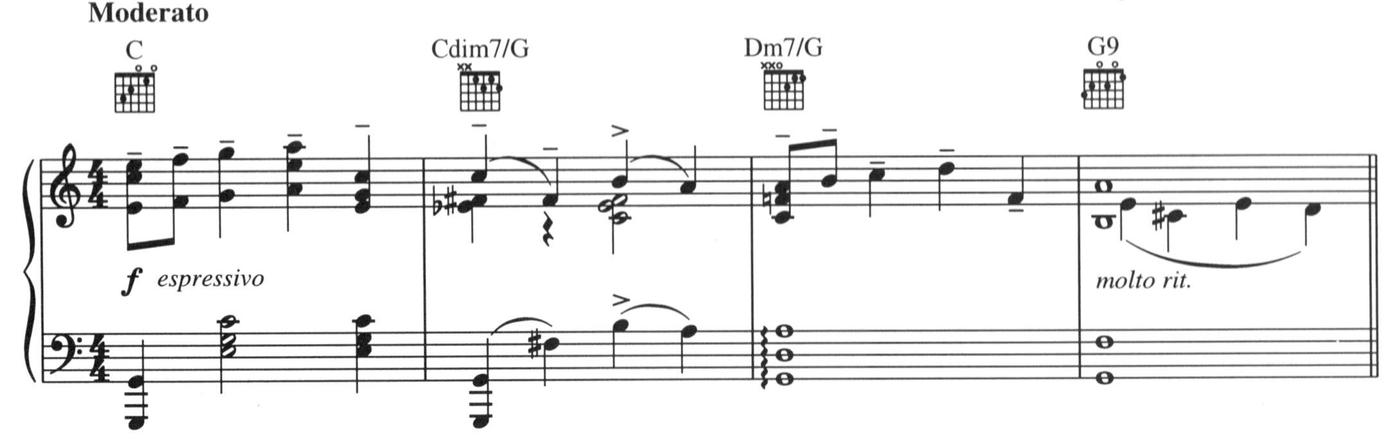

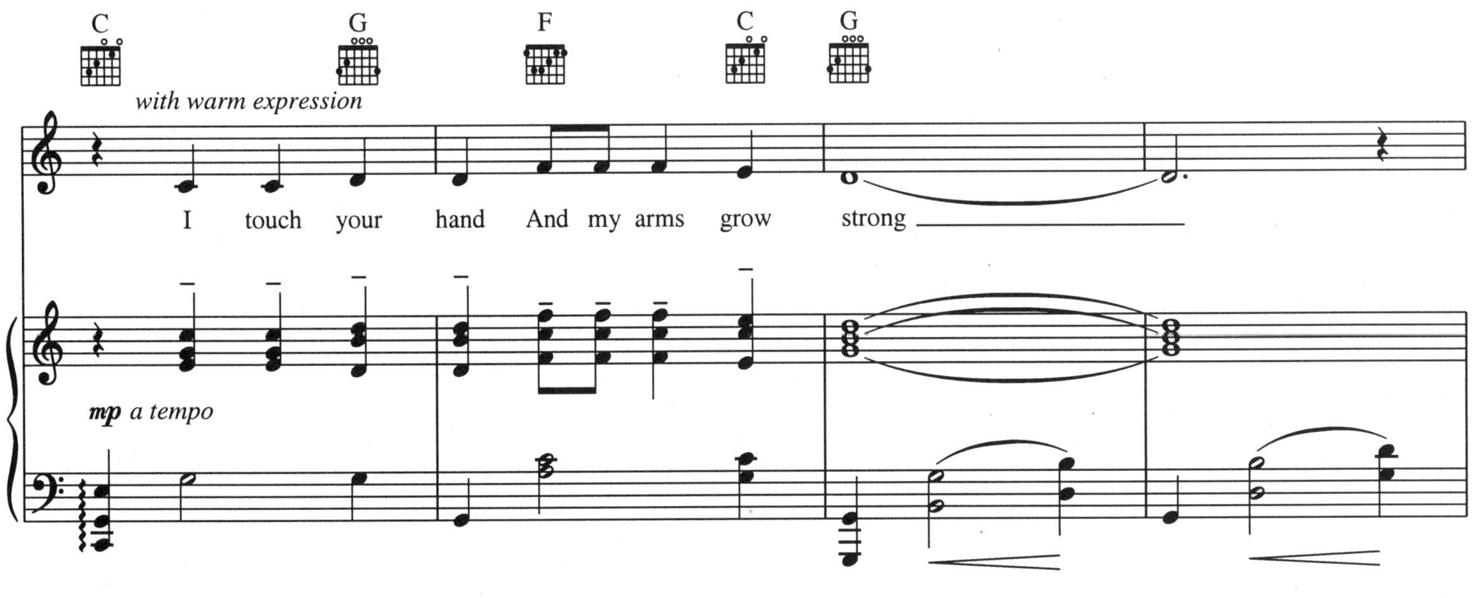

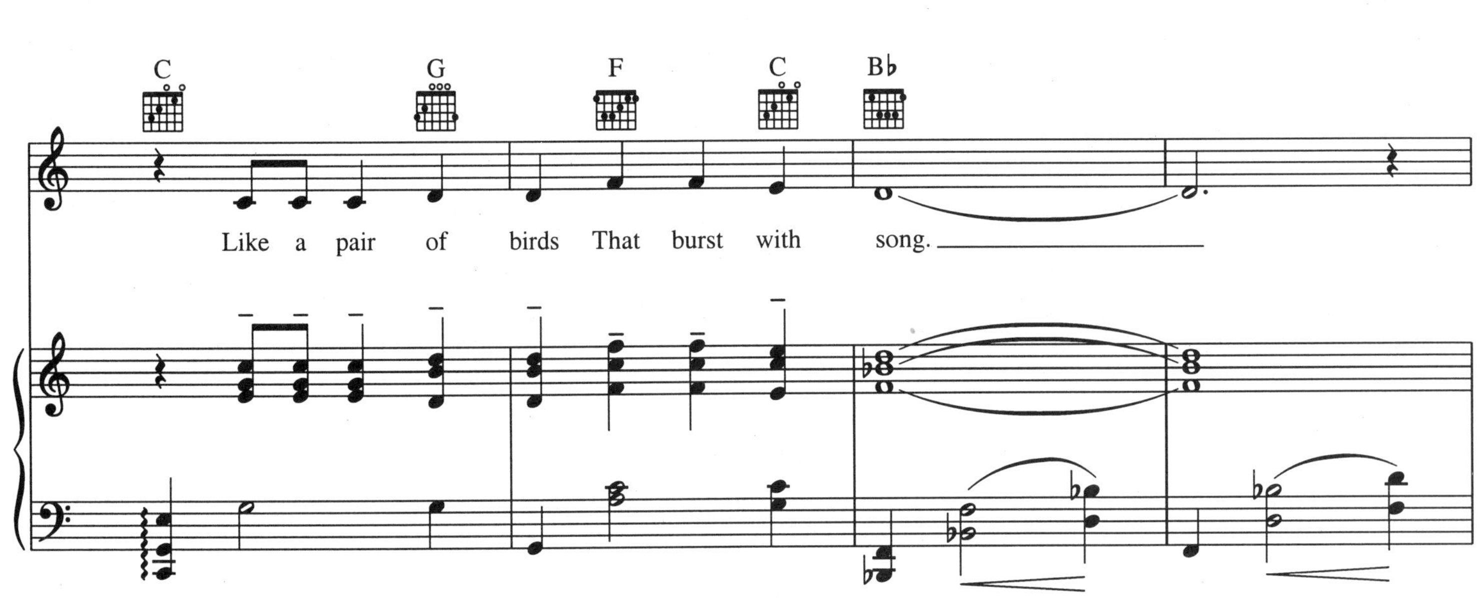

Dm
Gdim
A7♭9
3 fr
Dm
Fm6
My eyes look down At your love - ly face And I hold the
f
C
C♯dim7
Dm7
G7
world In my em - brace.
mf
molto rit.
Refrain (slowly, with great warmth)
C
G/B
Young - er than Spring - time are you, Soft - er than star - light
p - mf
C
Am
D
are you, Warm-er than winds of June are the gen - tle lips you

Gmaj7
G7
C
G/B
gave me. Gay - er than laugh - ter are you, Sweet - er than mu - sic
p
C
Am
D
are you, An - gel and lov - er, heav - en and earth are you to
(stay in slow tempo)
G
D7
G
D7
me. And when your youth and joy in - vade my
mf
cresc.
G
D7
G
Dm7
arms And fill my heart as now they do...

G7
C
G
C
G/B
then...
Young-er than Spring-time
am I,
Gay-er than laugh-ter
mp
C
G7/B
C
with passion
Am
am I,
An-gel and lov-er,
heav-en and earth am
cresc.
Am7/D
G7
1 C
G7
I
with
you!
f
allarg.
a tempo
2 C
you!
f dim.
morendo
p

YOU ARE BEAUTIFUL

from FLOWER DRUM SONG

Lyrics by OSCAR HAMMERSTEIN II
Music by RICHARD RODGERS

Refrain (tranquillo)
D6/9 D D6/9 D Em A
You are beau - ti-ful, small and shy. You are the girl whose
p dolce
F♯m/E G/A A Em A D D6/9 D
eyes met mine Just as your boat sailed by. This I know of you,
D6/9 D Em A F♯m/E G/A Em A9
noth - ing more, You are the girl whose eyes met mine Pass-ing the riv - er
D9 G D G D(add9)
shore. You are the girl whose laugh I heard, Sil-ver and soft and bright;
mf

G/B D/A E9 Em7/D A7 D6/9
4fr
Soft as the fall of lo - tus leaves Brush-in' the air of night. While your
p
D D6/9 D Em A F♯m/E G/A
4fr
flow - er boat sailed a - way, Gen-tly your eyes looked back on mine,
Em A7 D7sus D7 G
clear - ly you heard me say: "You are the girl I will
mf più espr.
A9 1 D A7sus A7 2 D
love some - day." day."
p
Ped.
*